A Saint-Saëns Organ Album

SELECTED AND ARRANGED BY MARTIN SETCHELL

MUSIC DEPARTMENT
OXFORD
UNIVERSITY PRESS

OXFORD
UNIVERSITY PRESS

Great Clarendon Street, Oxford OX2 6DP, England
198 Madison Avenue, New York, NY 10016, USA

Oxford University Press is a department of the University of Oxford.
It furthers the University's aim of excellence in research, scholarship,
and education by publishing worldwide

Oxford is a registered trade mark of Oxford University Press
in the UK and in certain other countries

First published 2006

1 3 5 7 9 10 8 6 4 2

ISBN 0-19-335592-2 978-0-19-335592-7

Music origination by
Enigma Music Production Services, Amersham, Bucks.
Printed in Great Britain on acid-free paper by
Halstan & Co. Ltd., Amersham, Bucks.

Contents

Introduction v

Notes on the pieces vi

Three pieces from *The Carnival of the Animals*

- The Elephant 1
- The Swan 4
- The Cuckoo 8

Danse Macabre, Op. 40 (extract) 11

O Salutaris hostia, from *Mass*, Op. 4 18

Two movements from 'Organ' Symphony No. 3, Op. 78

- Poco Adagio 21
- Maestoso (extract) 29

Pastorale, from *Oratorio de Noël*, Op. 12 34

Prelude to *Le Déluge,* Op. 45 38

Softly awakes my heart, from *Samson and Delilah*, Op. 47 46

Prière, Op. 158 50

Introduction

Camille Saint-Saëns (1835–1921) was a gifted concert pianist, organist, and scholar, as well as a skilled and prolific composer. As organist he served first at the Parisian church of St Merry (1853–7) and later at the Madeleine (1858–77). In early middle age, he resigned from regular church employment and devoted himself to composition and concert performance, largely thanks to a generous legacy.

His lifelong affection for the organ is evident from works such as the ever-popular 'Organ' Symphony No. 3, with its stirring melodies and famous sudden *forte* organ chord. Moreover, his orchestral scoring was often organ-influenced, even when the original did not include the organ, and thus much of his other music lends itself well to the instrument.

This volume of transcriptions brings some of his best-loved music to the organ. Included here are favourite movements from *The Carnival of the Animals*, the opening of the *Danse Macabre*, and sections of the 'Organ' Symphony. Also included are lesser-known works, all well-suited to the organ in style and mood.

Saint-Saëns' music ranges widely in style, and this too is illustrated in the volume. Note his warm, lyrical melodies ('Softly awakes my heart', 'The Swan', or the Andantino of the Prelude to *Le Déluge*), mastery of Baroque pastiche (the Pastorale and 'O Salutaris hostia'), consummate fugal technique (Prelude to *Le Déluge*), and near-Wagnerian chromaticism mixed with antique-sounding false relation (parts of the Prière).

In all, this volume presents a range of attractive arrangements for organ, from different genres and different periods of Saint-Saëns' life. The majority are suitable for both church and concert use. In his own words: 'He who does not feel wholly satisfied with elegant lines, harmonious colours, and a fine series of chords, does not understand art.' I hope that many players and listeners will enjoy exploring Saint-Saëns' art in these delightful pieces.

MARTIN SETCHELL

Notes on the pieces

Three pieces from *The Carnival of the Animals*

This witty and amusing Grand Zoological Fantasy was written for private performance in 1886, after which Saint-Saëns refused to allow either publication or performance (except of 'The Swan') until after his death in 1921. Perhaps he guessed how popular the work would become!

The Elephant

The original double-bass solo is given unaltered to the pedals. It needs clear and careful articulation, with as many heavy 8', 16', and even 32' foundation stops as necessary for the tune to dominate. The accompaniment is the original piano 2 part, thinned a little in texture for organ. The middle section (bars 21–36) uses the theme from the 'Ballet des Sylphes' by Berlioz at slow tempo, and should be more *legato*, suggesting the amusing picture of an elephant dancing in a ballet skirt.

The Swan

With its graceful, long-breathed melody (originally for cello) sailing serenely over the gently rippling accompaniment (two pianos), this must be the most famous and beautiful of all swan songs. The transcription is essentially the version prepared by Saint-Saëns' friend Alexandre Guilmant with some minor editorial changes (for example, the removal of the awkward pedal arpeggio in bar 24 and addition of the piano 2 full chord in the last bar, perhaps overlooked by Guilmant).

The Cuckoo

The full title is 'Le coucou au fond des bois' ('The cuckoo in the depths of the wood'). The clarinettist is directed to play 'dans la coulisse' (i.e. off-stage), to make the cuckoo-calls sound clear, yet distant, so organists should avoid too strident a solo. The thick texture of the original chordal accompaniment for two pianos is best represented by adding or deleting 4' and 16' stops as marked. The essential *legato* is most easily achieved by sharing the chords between the two hands where possible (as suggested in bar 1).

Danse Macabre, Op. 40

Written in 1874, Saint-Saëns' *Dance of Death* was inspired by the poem of Henry Cazalis, based on the old superstition that at Halloween, Death with his fiddle (the E string tuned to E flat) calls the skeletons from their graves to dance until dawn. It has become famous, not least through use in TV series such as *Buffy the Vampire Slayer* and *Jonathan Creek*. This transcription of the opening 137 bars includes the two main themes. Cues of the original instrumentation are given in brackets; these are not intended as registration suggestions, but players should bear them in mind in choosing appropriate, quick-speaking stops.

O Salutaris hostia, from the Mass in G minor, Op. 4

Saint-Saëns was appointed organist of St Merry in 1853 at the age of 18, but the Cliquot organ was virtually unplayable during the first four years of his tenure. The Mass was written to mark the re-opening of Cavaillé-Coll's rebuilt instrument in 1857. It is scored for 4 soloists, choir, strings, 2 flutes, 2 cor anglais, 3 trumpets, 3 trombones, harp, and 2 organs. The rebuilt Grand Orgue has independent solos, while the petit orgue doubles choral voice parts and is used in lighter texture movements, like this devotional aria, which was traditionally sung at the Elevation (between the Sanctus and the Agnus Dei). In this transcription the organ and harp parts are in the right hand and pedal, and the soprano solo, doubled by flutes and cor anglais, is in the left hand at 4' pitch.

Two movements from the 'Organ' Symphony No. 3 in C minor, Op. 78

This popular symphony was written for the Royal Philharmonic Society and premièred in 1886 in St James Hall, London, with the composer conducting.

Poco Adagio

The symphony's haunting slow movement features the organ in a quasi-continuo role, though occasionally with independent counterpoints. This transcription distinguishes between the principal melodic lines (usually marked solo) and secondary melodic strands, maintaining as much of the original organ part as possible. Memorable orchestral passages, rescored for organ solo, are the duo for first and second violins (bars 54–65) and the double-bass triplets, hinting at the symphony's main theme (bars 75–86). Saint-Saëns was clearly very fond of this movement, as he himself arranged it for four hands at two pianos, and there are several other piano arrangements.

Maestoso

In this famous finale, the theme is transformed into a triumphant chorale statement, after a brief introduction, launched by the big C major chord (incidentally marked *f*, not *fff*, but which sounds loud after the preceding *ppp*). This transcription comprises the first 24 bars, with the last 3 bars of the movement appended as a coda. It reflects the original scoring as far as possible: the *p* statement (bars 9–16) has the *legato* chorale theme for strings in the left hand with the piano arpeggios in the right, and the *ff* version has the full string chords in the left hand, the organ 'punctuations' in the right, and the brass fanfares allotted to solo reeds. Players may recognize this theme as used—and even sung by mice!—in the film *Babe*.

Pastorale, from *Oratorio de Noël*, Op. 12

Saint-Saëns' *Oratorio de Noël* (*Christmas Oratorio*) of 1858 is a gentle meditation with Latin text, doubtless intended for Midnight Mass at the Madeleine, and scored for four soloists, choir, strings, harp, and organ. This opening Prelude is sub-titled 'in the style of J. S. Bach' and its 12/8 meter (suggesting the rocking cradle), is a common feature of eighteenth-century pastoral Christmas music. This transcription reflects the original contrasting solo timbres of organ hautbois and first violins (a Great flute is suggested as a suitable replacement).

Prelude to *Le Déluge*, Op. 45

Written in 1875, *Le Déluge* (*The Flood*), subtitled 'Poème Biblique' is a short oratorio in three sections, recounting God's anger at Man's corruption, Noah and the flood, and His forgiveness, symbolized by the rainbow and the dove. The orchestral Prelude comprises a short introduction, followed by a strict fugue which melts into a lyrical Andantino in the tonic major. This *cantabile* theme continues immediately in Part 1, and depicts Man's idyllic state before corruption: happiness and prosperity, a land of sunshine, and the undefiled beauty of their daughters. This piece was obviously one of the composer's favourites, as he included it in several recital programmes (using a different transcription by Guilmant).

Softly awakes my heart, from *Samson and Delilah,* Op. 47

As a frequent visitor to England, Saint-Saëns was familiar with the English oratorio tradition and originally planned to use the biblical story of Samson as an oratorio. Instead he completed a three-act opera in 1877, the first and only one of his thirteen operas to achieve wide popularity, though it was not produced in France until 1890. In this famous aria from Act II (more accurately translated as 'My heart opens at your voice'), Delilah seductively demands that if he loves her, Samson must share with her the secret of his strength; he weakens and eventually succumbs (represented musically by his 'singing her tune' in duet). This transcription presents one statement of each of the solo sections plus a simple coda.

Prière, Op. 158

Together with *Cyprès et Lauriers*, Op. 156 for organ and orchestra, and the *Troisième Fantaisie*, Op. 157 for organ, this piece was one of Saint-Saëns' last works, written in 1919, just two years before his death. It was originally scored for cello and organ, then arranged for violin and organ the following year. This transcription follows the original closely, though its wide-ranging melody has necessitated some discreet octave transposition, and the accompaniment is slightly re-arranged for left hand and pedals where necessary (the designation 8' pedal indicates the original is for manuals only at that point).

The Elephant

from *The Carnival of the Animals*

CAMILLE SAINT-SAËNS
arr. Martin Setchell

Printed in Great Britain

OXFORD UNIVERSITY PRESS, MUSIC DEPARTMENT, GREAT CLARENDON STREET, OXFORD OX2 6DP

15

21

mp

[*simile*]

mf

26

31

cresc.

37
41
45
Gt. ff
49
8va (ad lib.)

The Swan

from *The Carnival of the Animals*

CAMILLE SAINT-SAËNS

arr. Alexandre Guilmant, ed. Martin Setchell

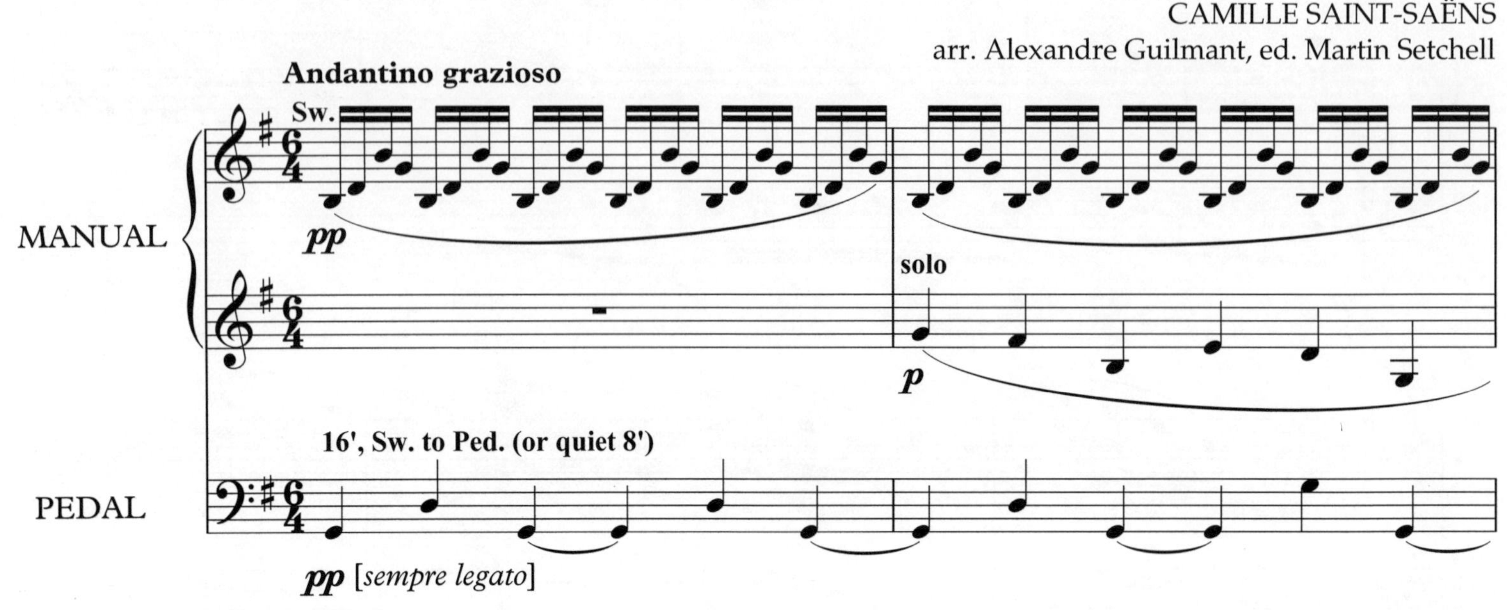

7
9
11
13
cresc.

15
dim.
cresc.
17
dim.
19
21

23

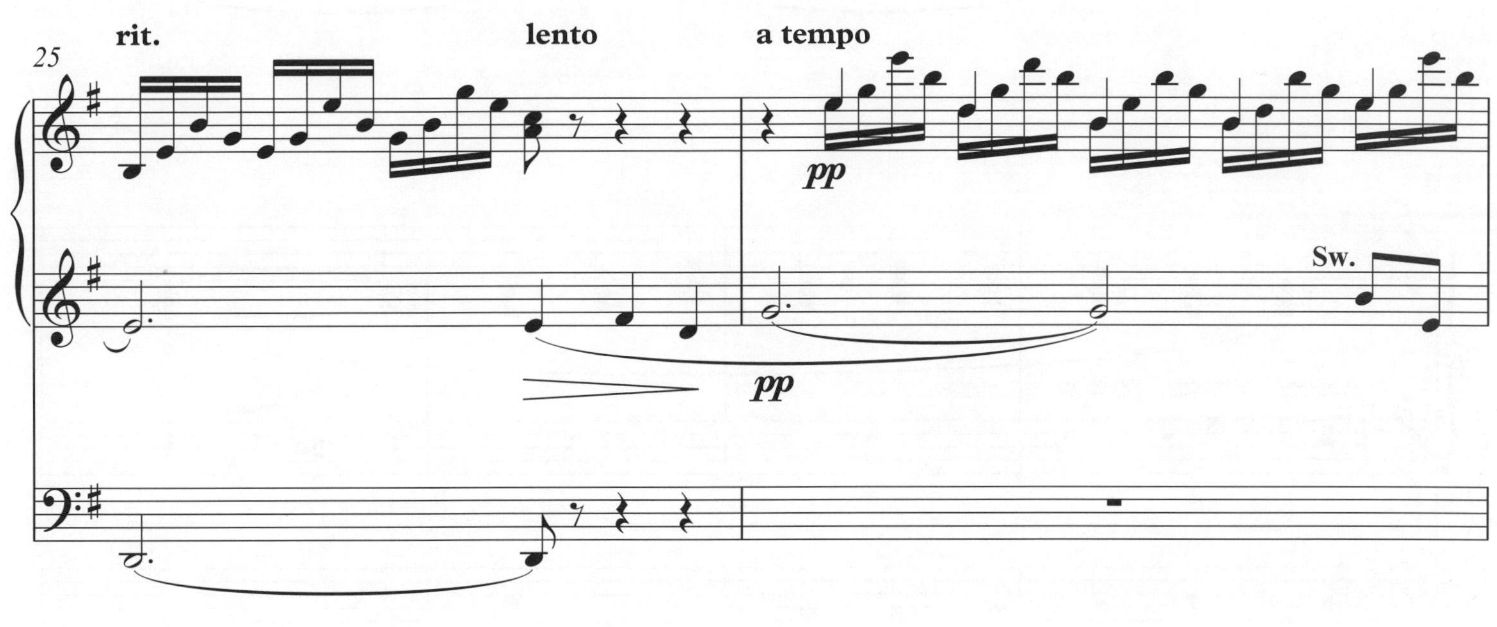
rit.
lento
a tempo
25
pp
Sw.
pp

27
rit.

The Cuckoo

from *The Carnival of the Animals*

CAMILLE SAINT-SAËNS
arr. Martin Setchell

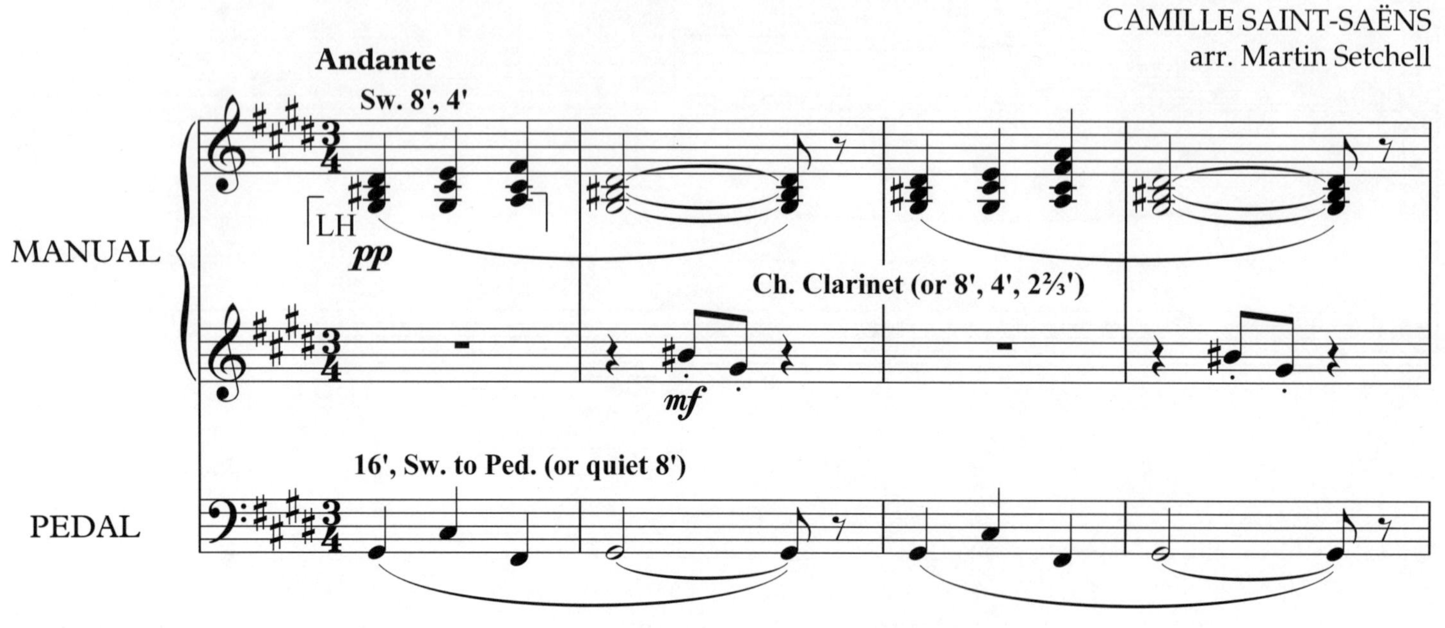

13

17

21

-16'

25

29
33
Sw.
solo
37
Sw.
solo
mp
40
Sw.
ppp
pp

Danse Macabre

Op. 40 (extract)

CAMILLE SAINT-SAËNS
arr. Martin Setchell

*Instrument designations in brackets are as the original scoring.

31
(tutti)
Sw. (solo flute)
p
Ch. (harp/strings)
pp
Gt. to Ped.
Ch. to Ped.
36
40
(violins)
pp
44

48
Gt.
(solo violin)
f largamente e marcato
53
58
63
(oboe/bassoon)
Sw.
p

67
Gt. (solo violin)
f

71
Sw. (flute/oboe/bassoon)
p

75
Gt. (solo violin)
f

79
Gt. ff

83
(tutti)
(violins)
Gt. to Ped.
88
92
8va (ad lib.)
f (WW/violin)
96
(8)

100
(8)
Gt.
+16' (violins, violas, cellos)
f
largamente e marcato
Ch.
Ch. to Ped.

105

110

115
-16' (solo violin)
f

120
8va (ad lib.)
Sw. (flute/clarinet)
124 (8)
Gt. (solo violin)
8va (ad lib.)
Sw. (flute/clarinet)
128
133 (8)
(solo violin)
Gt. ff
(tutti)
Gt. to Ped.

O Salutaris hostia

from *Mass*, Op. 4

CAMILLE SAINT-SAËNS
arr. Martin Setchell

11
Sw.
13
solo
16
18
Sw.
solo

21

24

26

Sw.

28

Poco Adagio

from 'Organ' Symphony No. 3, Op. 78

CAMILLE SAINT-SAËNS
arr. Martin Setchell

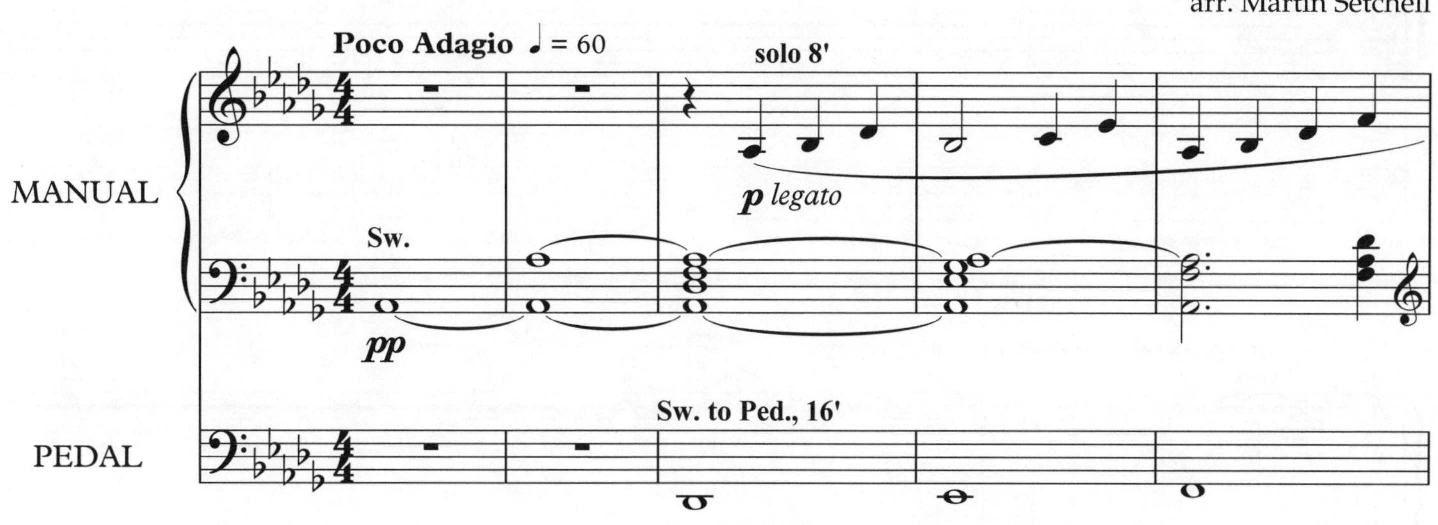

14
Sw.
Sw. +16'
p
Gt. 16', 8' (4')
p legato
p
19
23
sub. p
27
Sw.
solo 8'

32
cresc.
38
Sw. (add)
dim.
43
Gt. 8', 4' (Sw. coupled)
49
Sw.

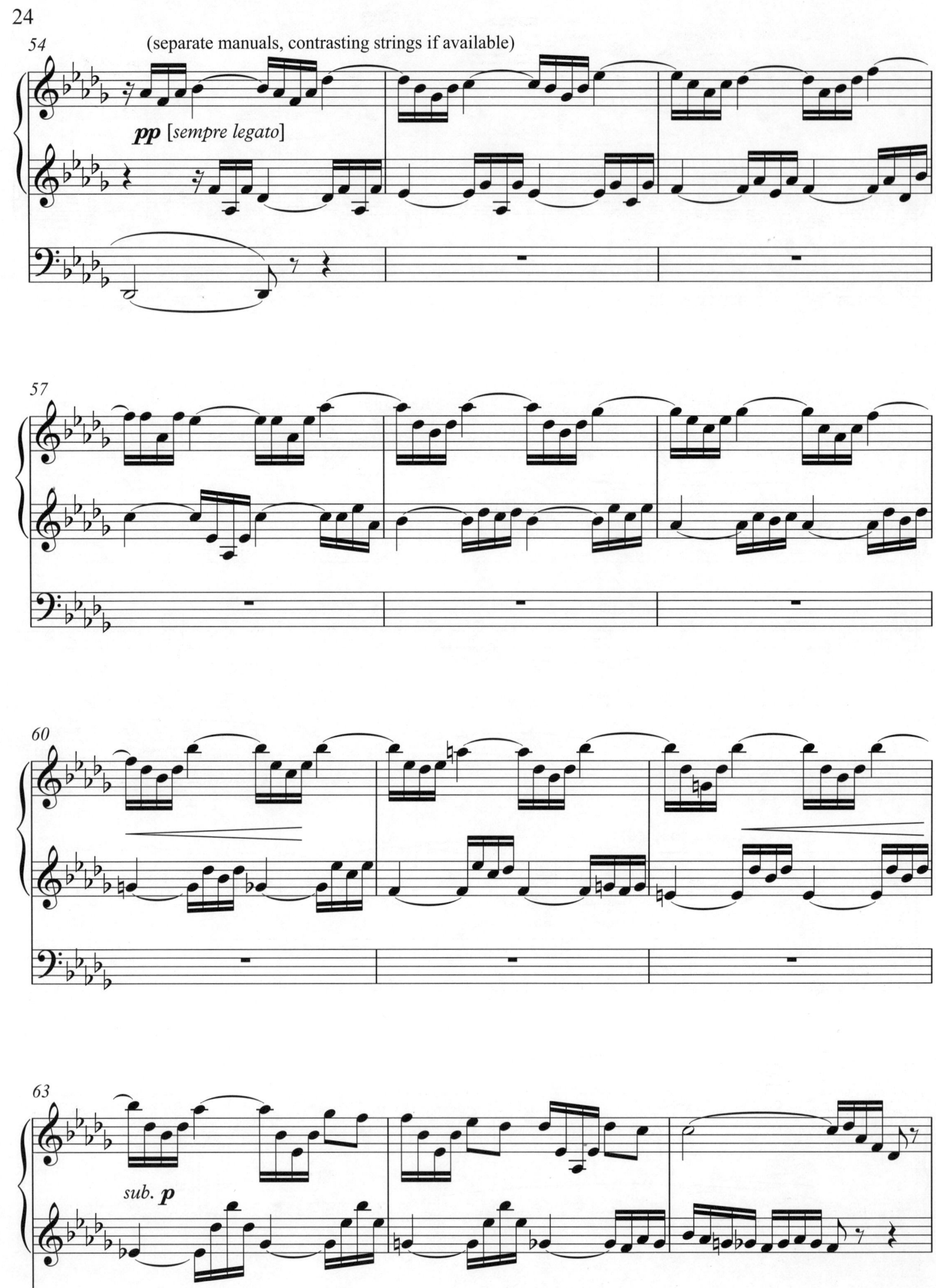
54
(separate manuals, contrasting strings if available)
pp [sempre legato]
57
60
63
sub. p

66
Gt., Sw. coupled
Sw. 16', 8'
69
8va (ad lib.)
cresc.
71
(8)
dim.
74
tr
Sw. p
soft 32', 16' uncoupled
p molto tranquillo
quasi pizz.

78
82
Gt. quasi pizz.
p
Sw.
85
Gt.
Sw.
Gt.
cresc.
88
Sw.
[p]
solo Gt. 16', 8', 4'
[mp] molto espressivo
Sw. to Ped.

92
97
cresc.
102
f Gt. (Sw. coupled)
+ Gt. to Ped.
8va (ad lib.)
solo 8' Flute
106
Sw.
dim.
Sw.
p
- Gt. to Ped.

111
contrasting colour
solo 8' Flute
115
contrasting colour
solo 8' Flute
Gt.
(Sw.)
espr.
Gt. to Ped.
120
pp
Sw. to Ped.
124
solo 8'
morendo

Maestoso

from 'Organ' Symphony No. 3, Op. 78 (extract)

CAMILLE SAINT-SAËNS
arr. Martin Setchell

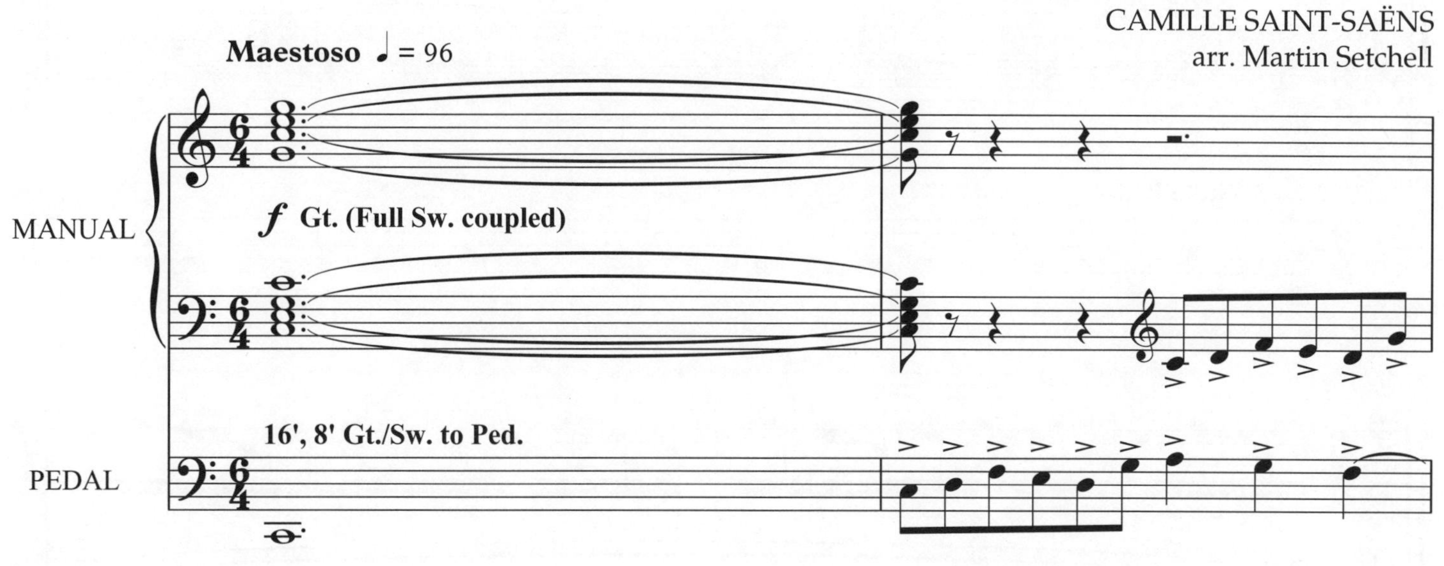

9
Sw. 8', 4', 2'
p
Ch. 8', 4'
- Gt. to Ped.
10
11
12

13
14
15
16

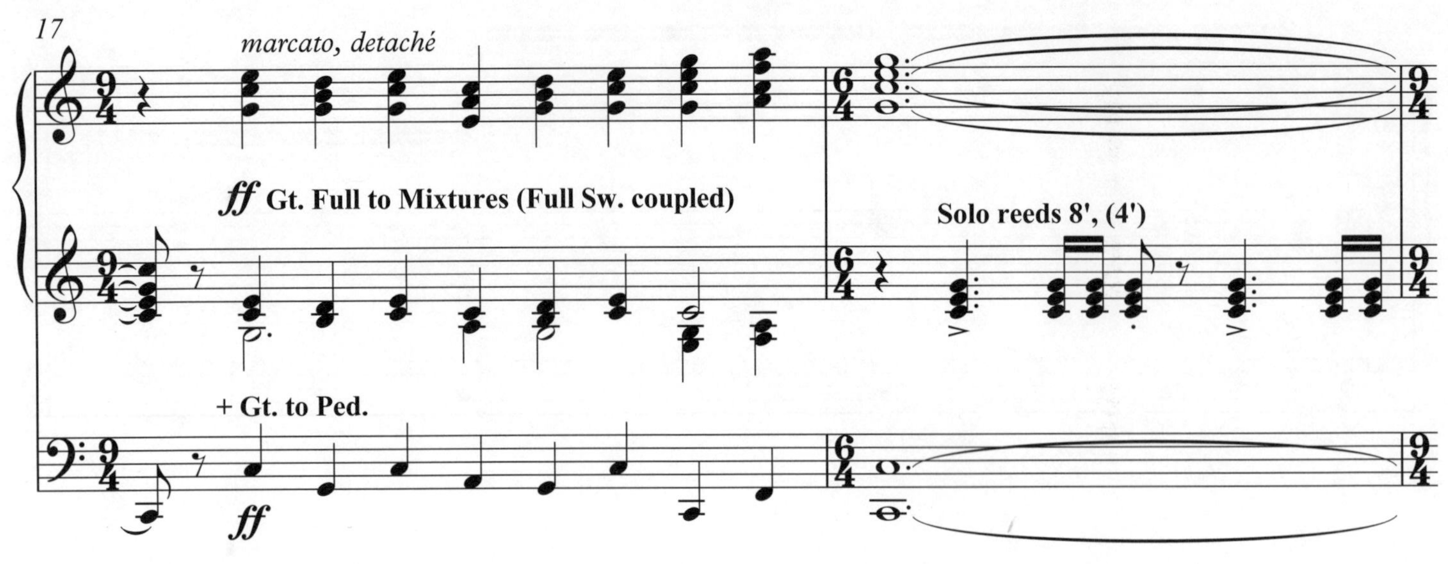
17
marcato, detaché
ff Gt. Full to Mixtures (Full Sw. coupled)
Solo reeds 8', (4')
+ Gt. to Ped.
ff

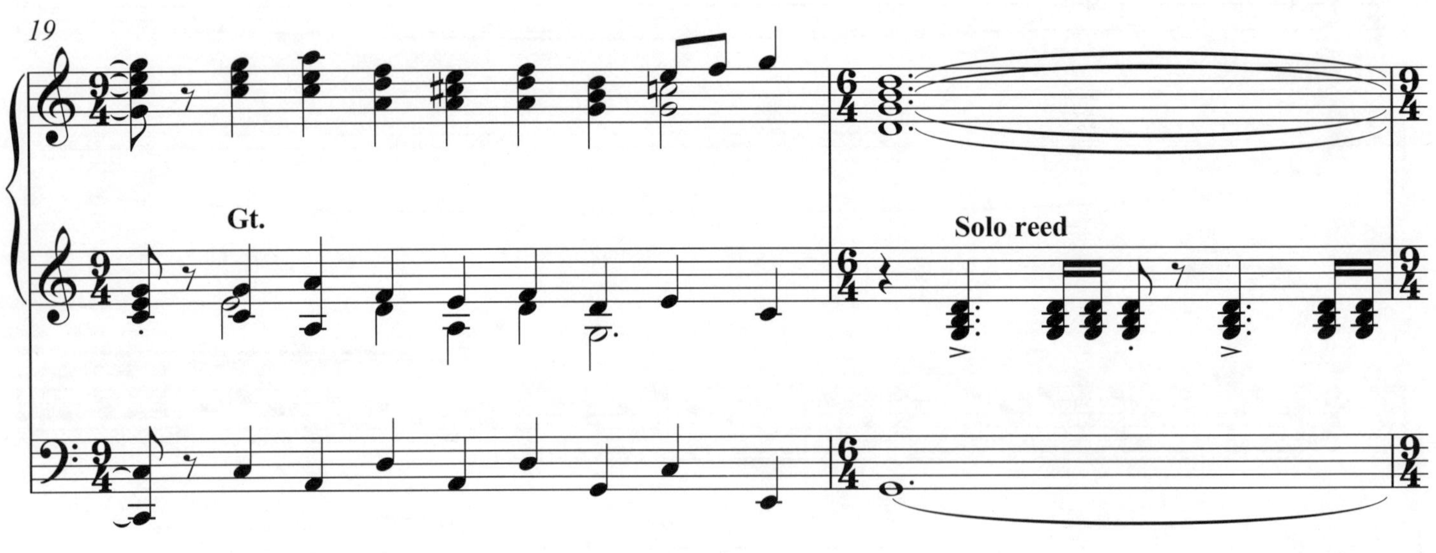
19
Gt.
Solo reed

21
Gt.
Solo reed

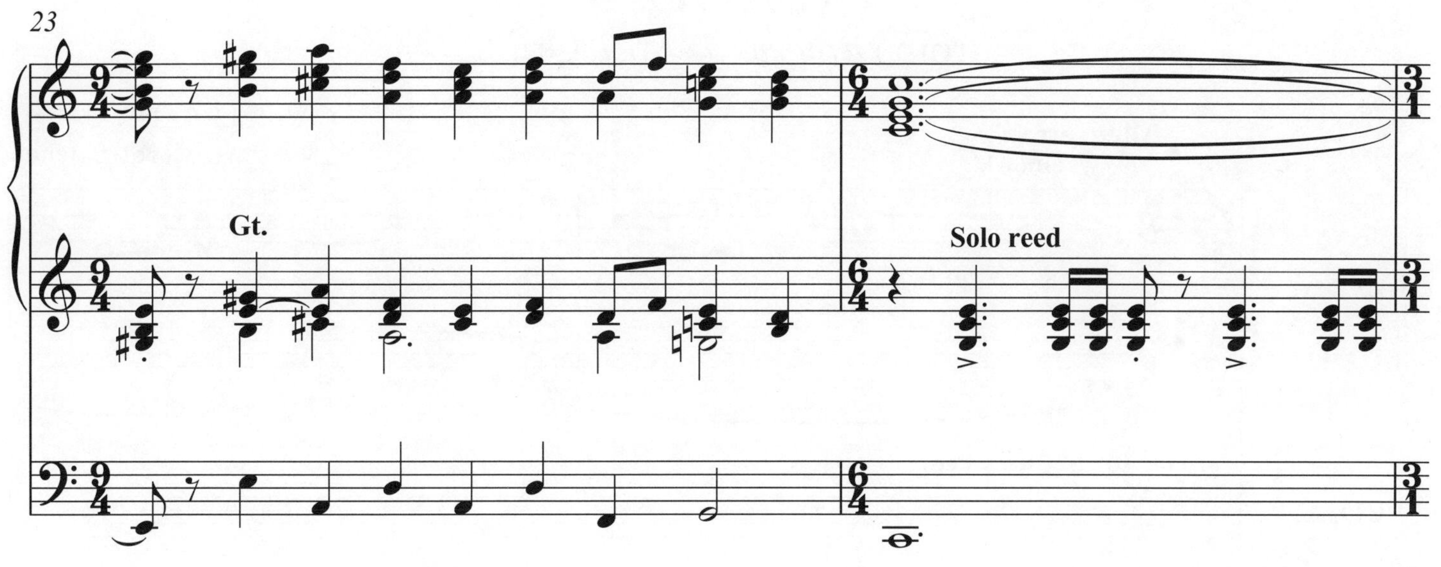
23
Gt.
Solo reed

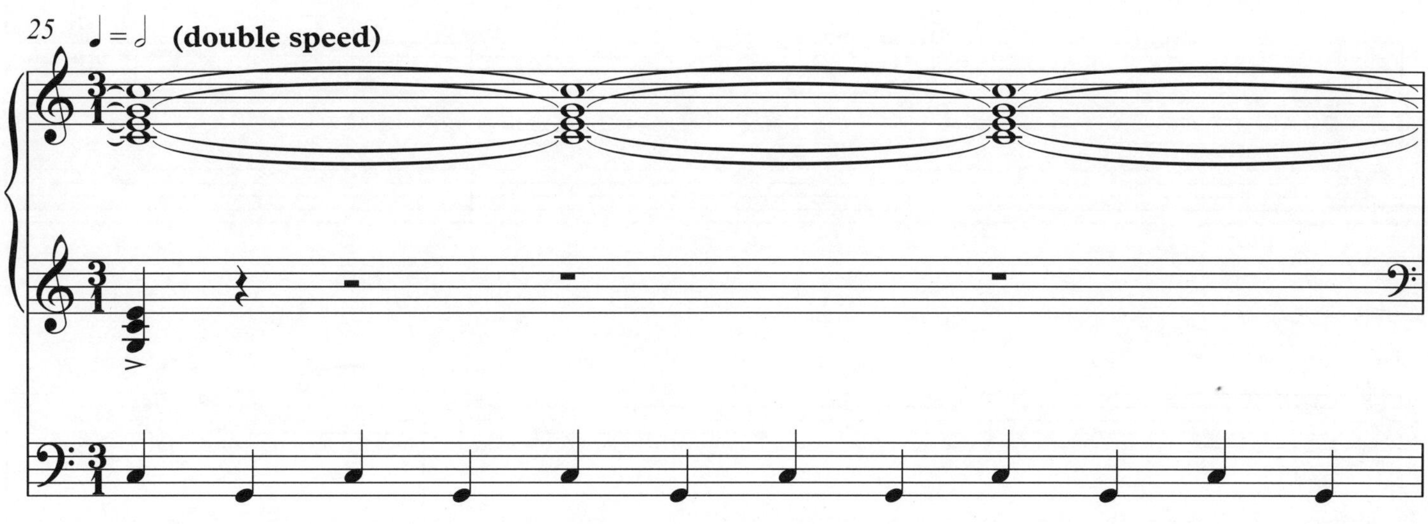
25
(double speed)

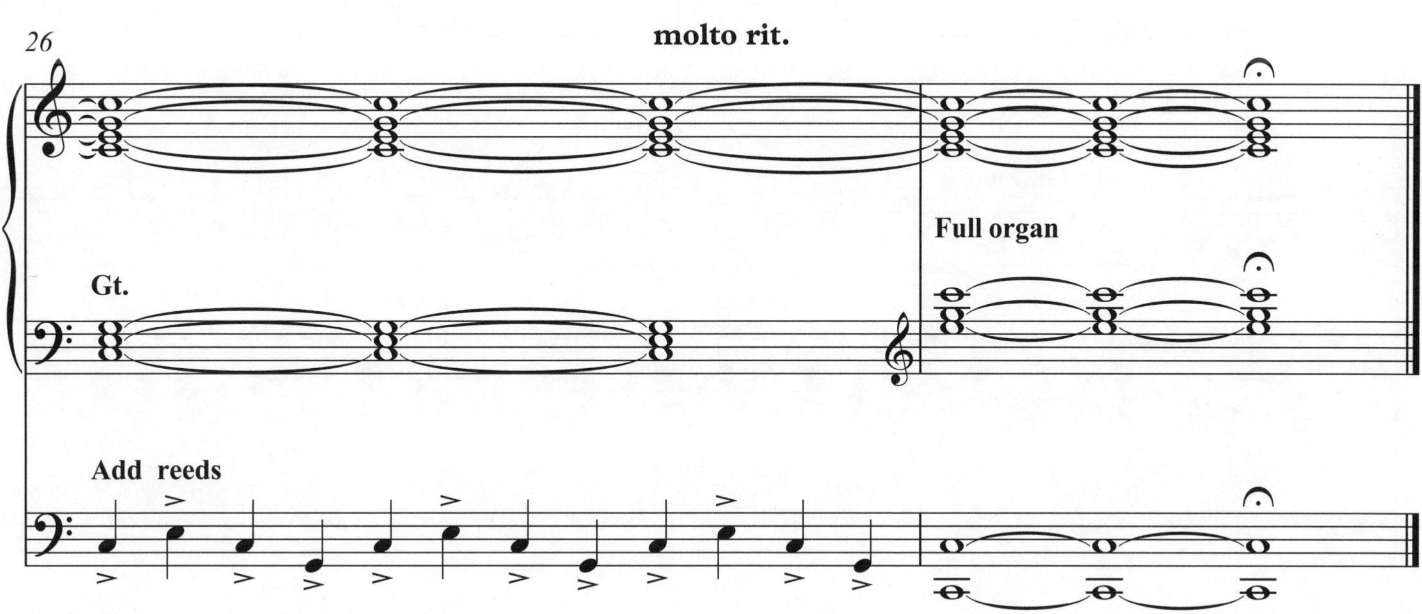
26
molto rit.
Gt.
Full organ
Add reeds

Pastorale

from *Oratorio de Noël*, Op. 12

CAMILLE SAINT-SAËNS
arr. Martin Setchell

12
cresc.
15
f
18
Sw. Oboe
f
21
p

25

cresc.

f

29

38
Gt. Flute
Ch.
41
Gt. Flute
Sw. Oboe
44
Gt. Flute (change to RH)
Gt. Flute
Sw. Oboe (change to LH)
Ch.
47

Prelude to *Le Déluge*

Op. 45

CAMILLE SAINT-SAËNS
arr. Martin Setchell

14
18
22
26

30
34
37
poco cresc.
40
poco a poco dim.

44
pp Sw.
- Gt. to Ped.
48
solo
52
pp
56
perdendosi

Andantino
solo
mp dolce
p

78
82
86
90

+16', or sub-octave coupler
94
mf
mp
98
102
cresc.
8va (ad lib.)
106
f
dim.

-16', or sub-octave coupler
p
ppp
RH thumb

Softly awakes my heart

from *Samson and Delilah*, Op. 47

CAMILLE SAINT-SAËNS
arr. Martin Setchell

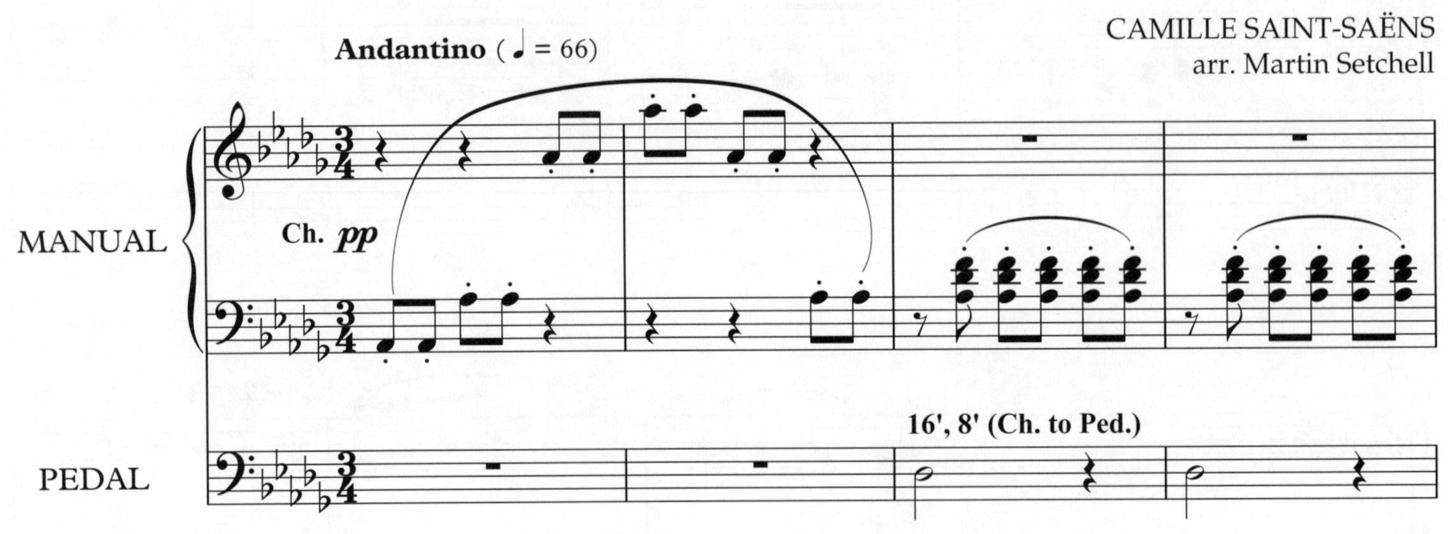

25
stringendo

29
mf

un poco più lento
32
dolce
pp

36
40
44
f
48
rit.
p
dim.
pp

Prière
Op. 158

CAMILLE SAINT-SAËNS
arr. Martin Setchell

13
f
[mp]
dim.
17
p
21
25

30
cresc.
35
mf
+16'
40
44
8' only

48
p
52
molto espressivo
56
60

64
cresc.

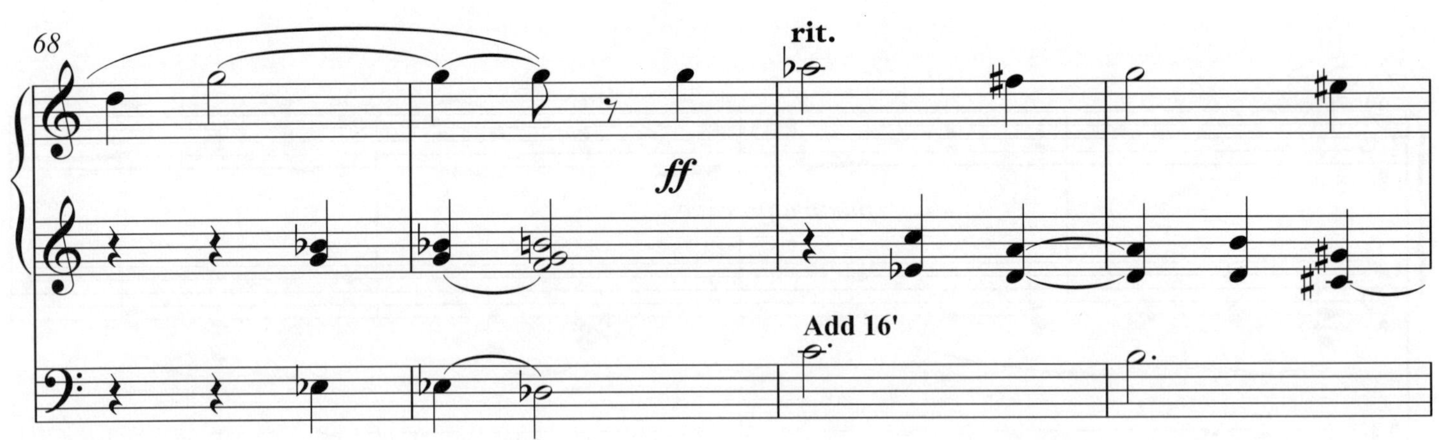
68
rit.
ff
Add 16'

72
poco rit.
lento
- 16'

Tempo I (Andante)
76
p
pp

80
molto espress.
84
88
cresc.
92
f
tranquillo

96

p

100

mf

104

più lento

pp

108

rit.

+16'

pp